Dealing with Death:
A Strategy for Tragedy

by
Evelyn B. Kelly

Library of Congress Catalog Card Number 90-62023
ISBN 0-87367-306-9
Copyright © 1990 by the Phi Delta Kappa Educational Foundation
Bloomington, Indiana

This fastback is sponsored by the Ball State University Chapter of Phi Delta Kappa, which made a generous contribution toward publication costs.

Table of Contents

Table of Contents

Introduction

Item: James, a popular seventh-grader, told his social studies teacher, "My head is pounding." The teacher, known for not letting kids out of class, told him to sit down. A few minutes later he came back to the teacher and told her his head was really killing him and that he wanted to check out of school. James' mother, a nurse, came after him, gave him an aspirin, and put him to bed. When she checked on him 30 minutes later, James was dead. Autopsy revealed a brain aneurysm.

Item: Bob and Billy were playing "war" with the neighborhood gang. Bob was wielding a real gun (unloaded, he thought) owned by his father. As he pulled the trigger, 11-year-old Sam ran in front of the gun. Sam died before the children's eyes. The neighborhood became a hysterical scene.

Item: A school bus specially designed for handicapped children traveled along a rural Florida road delivering students home after a long day. A logging truck approached an intersection and ran the stop sign. The next day's headlines read, "Semi Truck Kills Nine on School Bus." The untold grief experienced by classmates of these students did not make the newspapers.

Rare and unusual happenings? No! Each year tragedies of this kind are reported in some newspaper almost daily. In 1987 some 8,000 children under the age of 14 were killed in accidents. According to Emergency Medical Services of Florida, the major causes of deaths in children are accidents, drownings, poisonings, and burns. Killings with guns became such a problem in Florida that a special session of the legislature enacted a stringent child protection gun law. Leaving a loaded weapon where a child may reach it is a criminal offense with a possible jail term.

According to the National Organization for Victim Assistance (quoted in Crase and Hamrick 1989), the annual incidence of violence in the U.S. includes nearly 50,000 murders and drunken driving fatalities. AIDS deaths have become a stark reality touching many students and their families. The evening TV news regularly carries stories — often in graphic detail — of catastrophic deaths resulting from airplane crashes, explosions, or earthquakes.

Some time ago the author attended a seminar for law enforcement officers conducted by MADD (Mothers Against Drunk Driving). The instructor asked the officers to describe how they felt the first time they had to tell a family of the death of a loved one. Their response was, "Inadequate, didn't know what to say." She then asked them to describe how they felt about their most recent experience of reporting a death to a family. The response was the same, "Inadequate, didn't know what to say."

If veteran law enforcement officers who deal with tragedy in the regular course of their work feel inadequate, how will teachers cope in the classroom when faced with an occasional tragedy? Most will likely respond in the same way as the law enforcement officers, "Inadequate, didn't know what to say."

When Pratt, Hare, and Wright (1987) interviewed 96 early childhood educators about their comfort level in discussing death with young children, most stated they did not feel prepared to discuss the subject either informally or formally. Particularly difficult for these teachers was dealing with the death of parents or close relatives or the death of a child in a class. Teachers of older students would likely express the same feelings of inadequacy.

What would you do tomorrow in your classroom if a tragedy were to strike one of your students? The intent of this fastback is to give educators a strategy for dealing with tragedy. It addresses the following questions:

1. What should principals and teachers do when a tragedy occurs to one of their students?
2. How can educators understand and express their grief?
3. How do students of different age levels respond to loss?
4. How do we deal with the mourning student?
5. What other sources of help may be available?

Responses to these questions are based on my review of the literature; from interviews with grief counselors, school counselors, and educators; and from discussions with parent groups. In this fastback, I do not deal with death education as a formal part of the curriculum, although I strongly support it.

When Tragedy Strikes

When tragedy strikes, how will you respond? Mary Ann Sinkkonen (1989), an elementary principal in Novato, California, faced such a situation. She received word before school that one of her students was seriously ill. After school closed that day, she called the student's home and was told that the student had died of "natural causes." "When I hung up the phone, I began to make a list of what to do," Sinkkonen said.

Faced with pulling together an organized response to such an incident, Sinkkonen found few places to turn for help. She knew many other educators have faced similar situations, so she decided to share what she learned from her experience. What follows is a common-sense approach to dealing with tragedy adapted from Sinkkonen's ideas plus some from the Marion County (Florida) Crisis Response Team Memorandum.

Get accurate information from primary sources. When tragedy strikes, rumors become rampant. Head them off by getting specific information from family members or from someone close to the family. In the incident cited earlier about James, the seventh-grader who died of an aneurysm, panic struck the community. There were rumors that he had a contagious encephalitis. Parents bombarded the school board with phone calls insisting they close the school. The local health department had to answer hundreds of calls about contagious diseases. No one knew anything.

Alert the teaching staff and provide them with accurate information about the death. Teachers need to be informed as soon as possible. Use a telephone tree to notify faculty before arrival at school or place information in their mailboxes and have a resource person nearby to answer questions. If time permits, call a brief faculty meeting before teachers have to face students. Follow up after school with a short meeting for an update and discussion of students' reactions to the tragedy.

Call the district superintendent. The superintendent is likely to receive calls from parents or board members and needs accurate information in order to respond. As more information becomes available, provide an update.

Develop a written response for telephone calls to the school. The school secretary or anyone else who answers the school telephone should have a written statement to read so that a consistent message is conveyed to all who call.

Contact local agencies for grief counseling and educational materials. Some agencies that can help are MADD (Mothers Against Drunk Driving), Hospice, Compassionate Friends (an organization of parents whose children have died), or the local mental health organization. Some agencies have grief counselors who will volunteer to work with students.

Contact the district's special services personnel and request they be at school the first day after the tragedy occurs. Educators who have experienced such tragedies emphasize that the first day is the worst, and they need all the support they can get. School psychologists and school nurses should be available. Some school systems are developing crisis teams to go out to schools when tragedies occur.

Involve parents. Contact key parents in the PTA or who serve on school advisory committees and develop with them a statement that they can read to other parents using a telephone tree. This can stave off the rumor mill as well as provide information for parents so they can discuss the tragedy with their children before they come to school.

Develop a letter to be sent to parents and other community members that is informative and reassuring. Some schools have meetings for parents or send out materials to alert parents about grief behaviors they might expect from their children and about ways of coping with the tragedy at home.

Arrange for released time for staff who may want to visit the family or attend the funeral service.

Allow students to attend the funeral service if they wish to do so. Students should be accompanied by their parents or other designated adult. Teachers should not accept this responsibility.

Do something immediately for the family. Write a letter to the student's family from the staff. Arrange to have prepared meals delivered to the family. People want to do something but often feel helpless in these situations. Asking them to help through a concrete collective action helps in the healing process.

Have a policy in place for dealing with the media. While the school has a responsibility to respond promptly to inquiries from the media, it also has an obligation to protect the privacy of students, parents, and staff. Designate one person to handle media inquiries and establish a location for their briefings. Make sure your information is accurate. If your school system has a public information officer, let that person deal with the media. If a reporter appears at school, a staff member should accompany him or her at all times. Ask reporters to respect the sensitivity of those touched by the tragedy. Decline requests for students to be interviewed during school hours. Also, inform staff members that they do not have to submit to being interviewed unless they choose to.

Joseph Franson (1988) describes a tragic incident in his high school where one weekend a popular girl was murdered by her boyfriend, also a well-liked student. "The media provided one of the thorniest problems during the entire process," said Franson. He described how one youthful-looking TV reporter went into the girls' locker room and recorded students' conversations. When groups of grieving students were shown on the six o'clock news that evening, he realized belatedly that students' privacy must be protected.

Ask the librarian to collect books dealing with loss and death. Make the books available to teachers for classroom use. Then after a week or so, let the students check out the books for personal reading. Several lists of books and resources are available. (See References, particularly Wass citations.)

Plan a school memorial. This can be a tree planting, a memorial bench, or scholarship established in the student's name. Flying the school flag at half staff is also appropriate. A school memorial serves as a type of closure to a formal period of mourning.

No one likes the thought of planning for tragedy, but it does happen when we least expect it. The ideas suggested above can serve as the basis for a strategy for tragedy. The sections that follow will develop some of these ideas more fully.

The Staff Peer Conference

Teachers and principals often have close personal ties to their students. It is important to consider their emotional needs at the time of a student death and to provide them an opportunity to talk through their own feelings before dealing with their students' reactions in the classroom. The principal or counselors might initiate the peer conference session, or a group of teachers might do it on their own. A professional grief counselor might be invited to serve as a resource person during the session.

The staff peer conference serves several purposes:

1. Staff can support each other in their grieving. Their responses to the tragedy will vary. Some may become very emotional; others will exhibit little outward emotion, but this does not mean they are any less affected by the tragedy. The death of a student arouses a complex set of emotions, which are expressed in a variety of ways.

Sally Karioth, a professor at Florida State University, is a death counselor who has worked with many schools at times of tragedy. In her book, *If You Want to Know You're Dying, Ask the Cleaning Lady* (1985), she describes the common stages of grief but emphasizes the stages go back and forth and may vary with individuals. The stages of grief are expressed in the following ways:

- Shock and numbness. These feelings occur at the time of loss and may last a few days or a few months.

- Denial. Persons don't want to believe what has happened. Statements heard commonly are, "This can't be true" or "I just can't believe it."
- Realization and emotional release. Persons feel the impact of the loss and an overwhelming sadness envelops them. Talking about the loss is vital as a form of emotional release.
- Disorganization and anxiety. Persons are in a state of confusion; forgetfulness is common.
- Depression and loneliness. Persons feel a loss of self-worth and need someone to listen to them.
- Guilt. Persons go through an "if only" phase trying to undo what has happened.
- Anger, frustration, and resentment. Persons must be told that these emotions are acceptable and must find expression for the sake of the sufferer's mental health.
- Reorganization and recovery. Life is not the same after a loss, but persons come to accept it and move on to normal routines of living.

In her classes Karioth often asks, "How long do you think the grieving process lasts?" Most students say two to six weeks — maybe a couple of months. However, researchers have found the grieving process can last as long as one to three years, sometimes longer. The point is, a grieving staff and their students cannot be expected to bounce back the next day as if nothing has happened.

2. Staff can discuss how they can assist students by serving as role models during the grieving process. Children learn by observing how significant adults in their lives handle grief, and they come to understand that the strong emotions associated with grief are normal. Mourning does not have to be hidden.

3. Staff can work out a plan for presenting the news of the tragedy to students and share ideas on how to cope with students' reactions. Grief counselors recommend that students to be told the news by their

teachers in the classroom rather than over the school's public address system.

4. Staff can review how children of different age levels will react to the news of a death. Children's concepts of death will vary with age, as will their ways of responding to it.

5. The staff should realize that the one thing they cannot do is plan a normal day. It is unrealistic to pretend nothing happened. Teachers should postpone major tests but structure the day, taking their cues from the students as to when to discuss the death and what to do.

The staff peer conference can be a very helpful experience for making it through that first day.

Dealing with Death at Different Age Levels

Opinions differ as to exactly when a child begins to comprehend the concept of death. One researcher places it at about two to three years old. Others say late three to four. As with most aspects of human development, it will vary among individuals. What is certain is that childrens' concepts of death change as they mature. Therefore, when discussing death, teachers must be cognizant of children's developmental level regarding concepts about death and vocabulary related to death. Piaget's cognitive developmental stages are helpful in this regard.

At the preoperational stage (approximately ages 2-6), children hold animistic ideas attributing life to inanimate objects and believe death is reversible. At this stage children are egocentric and assume everyone sees the world as they do. At the concrete operational stage (ages 7-11), children see their world in terms of real objects and are concerned with the mechanical aspects of how things work. They understand that death is irreversible. At the formal operational stage (ages 12 and up), students are capable of thinking logically and abstractly. They understand cause-and-effect relationships.

Teacher Suggestions for the Preoperational Stage

When telling children at this stage about a death, you should speak simply and truthfully about what has happened. For example, "Jamie was killed in a car accident last night. The doctors and nurses tried to help him, but they could not." Also let the children know how you feel. "I am very sad and my feelings are all mixed up right now. Each of you may have different kinds of feelings. I want you to tell me what you are thinking. I will try to answer what you ask." Tell them crying is okay. Not crying is okay. "Feeling bad inside is okay. After a while, you will feel better."

By sharing your feelings of grief and sadness, you are modeling a natural response to death. Take your cues from the children, who in time will indicate what comfort they need and what information they can handle.

Keep in mind that children at this developmental stage do not accept death as permanent. To them anything that is active is alive; a wind-up toy moves and therefore is alive. To them death is not forever. After all, the coyote on the "Roadrunner" TV cartoon show gets flattened and then jumps right back up again. E.T. came back to life. They see death on television but seldom realize its finality.

Children may appear to accept the news of a tragedy in a matter of fact manner. After all, the missing one will be back. Expect questions about the person's return. You may explain, "His body was badly hurt. The doctors could not fix it. It stopped working. He is dead."

Young children think big people are omnipotent. Do not tell them half-truths or use euphemisms about death in order to protect them. Do not say the deceased child has gone on a trip or moved. By the child's logic, big people can bring them back if they want to.

Young children will likely have difficulty articulating their grief. This may be their first experience with death, and they cannot express what they want to say. When talking to them, bend down to make eye contact. Expect some unusual questions, which may be asked over and over again. Do not laugh at their questions or consider them cute or dumb. The important thing when answering their questions is to be truthful.

Here are some questions one might hear from preschool children:

Who deaded him?
When will Sharon come back?
Can David still eat dinner? ice cream?
Do horses die? What about tigers?

Be aware that young children often express their feelings through fantasy play. This is healthy and should not be discouraged. Karioth tells of a frantic call she received from a kindergarten teacher. After Jenny, a child in her class, had been murdered, the children made a coffin out of their blocks and took turns lying in it. When Karioth arrived at the classroom, she asked, "Say, what's going on here?" (She already knew.) A boy occupying the coffin at that moment looked up and asked, "When is Jenny coming back?" What seemed to the teacher like macabre behavior was actually normal play activity for these children, and the question the boy asked was quite typical for this age level.

Children at this age also make connections between death and other events in their life experience that seem unusual to adults. For example, a six-year-old's brother and sister were killed in a drunk driving accident. About a month later the police found the boy lying on the highway trying to be hit so he could be with his brother and sister. A child was told Mary died of a headache. She hears her mother say she has a headache and wonders whether she will die too. Or a child hears people say old people die. From the child's perspective her daddy is old. Will he die soon?

The examples above point up the need for explaining death in very concrete terms. "A very bad thing happened last night to John. He was hit by a car. His body stopped working and it won't work anymore. The body cannot move, walk, see, hear; none of the parts work any more. He cannot eat or drink." Use words like "dead," "stopped working," "wore out." Avoid euphemisms like "passed away," "left us," "gone on," or "went to sleep." Young children take such words literally, and to them they imply the person is taking a trip and will return.

Young children also indulge in a type of magical thinking. They believe that what they wish or say will actually happen. For example, they said something bad to a classmate or wished that person were dead, so they caused the death. They also may think that by wishing they can bring the dead person back to life.

Teacher Suggestions for the Concrete Operational Stage

By the age of seven or eight, children are entering Piaget's concrete stage and are beginning to understand that death is final and irreversible. Many will become fearful when they realize this for the first time. They begin to wonder what happens after death, so be prepared for questions about their own death. They may see death as the Grim Reaper, someone who comes to get you, or maybe something you catch like a cold. On the other hand, children this age can readily comprehend death resulting from accidents, because they have been warned repeatedly in school and at home about the hazards of crossing the street, swimming without supervision, and playing with guns.

Teachers and classmates make up a child's second family. When tragedy happens, all are a part. The classroom provides a safe and caring setting where sharing grief benefits the entire class.

After sharing your own feelings with the students, explain that the emotions they are feeling are okay. Crying (yes, even for boys and men), feeling bad, frightened, or angry is okay. There is no right or wrong way to express grief. Children will do what makes them feel best. Don't make them assume a sadness they do not feel. You are giving students permission to talk about their feelings. Your modeling gives their feelings validity. Some children may want to talk and ask questions about the tragic event; some may never mention it again. Some children may resolve their grief in a few days; others may take weeks or months.

Be prepared for surprises. The child you expect to be the most vocal may be unusually quiet. In a fourth-grade class the teacher was discussing gun safety after a student had been accidentally shot by another student. A boy in the class suddenly raised his hand and blurted out, "My mother was killed by a gun." The teacher was not aware that the boy's mother had committed suicide when he was in the second grade. A little later this boy went into a rage, stabbing a teacher intern with his pencil. His pent-up rage had been set off by the discussion of the shooting incident and gun safety. He had never been allowed to deal with his grief.

The above incident is an extreme case, but there is likely to be a lot of free-floating anger at the time of tragedy. Students might be more irritable, impatient, fly off the handle, or cry without provocation. Psychologists say such emotions arise because students feel powerless to prevent the tragedy. When students are in such moods, do not try to cheer them up. Acknowledge their anger. Say, "You seem so angry. What happened is scary for all of us." Children are resilient; most will adjust to the loss over time.

Advise parents that they may see emotional swings in their children after a tragedy. Eating patterns may change. Lack of appetite is a common reaction, as is insomnia. Early childhood fears may resurface, such as fear of the dark, fear of thunderstorms, fear of a loved one dying. In Tallahassee when two boys returning from a miniature golf game were killed by a drunk driver, the principal sent all parents a brochure titled, "Your Child and Grief," which explained what to expect in their children's behavior and discussed some elements of the grief process.

You also may see "survivor guilt" in students. They may blame themselves for things that had nothing to do with the tragedy. For example, John is upset because he had been mean to Jerry just the day before the fatal accident. In such cases simply say, "This is not your fault. Maybe what you said was not nice, but you are not responsible for what happened."

Avoid getting into religious beliefs about death and the afterlife. Such concepts as "heaven," "soul," and "God's will" are better left to clergy to explain. However, the children will no doubt discuss these ideas among themselves. If the topic of religious beliefs comes up, simply state that people have different beliefs and tell students to discuss it with their parents and clergy.

Most death counselors agree that older children should be allowed to visit the funeral home and attend the funeral service if they want to. This is a decision parents should make with their children, and they should attend with them. The teacher might explain what the students will see and how they should conduct themselves. Describe the flowers, the coffin, the pall bearers, and something about the roles of the funeral director and clergy. Students this age are often curious about the details of internment, so a brief description of the procedures would be appropriate.

When a classmate dies, let students do something. Have them write cards and notes to the bereaved family. Encourage them to keep a journal of their feelings and illustrate it with drawings or pictures. Do a "Thanks for the Memories" book of poems, letters, and drawings. One school has a memorial garden where trees are planted in memory of students who die. These kinds of activities give students a tangible way to say goodbye. If a student is killed by a drunk driver or by a gun, organize a student letter-writing campaign to legislators demanding that they enact more stringent laws to curb such tragedies. Such an activity can be a powerful lesson in citizenship education.

Reading books that deal with death can be excellent therapy. (See fastback 151 *Bibliotherapy: The Right Book at the Right Time*.) Leo Buscaglia's *The Fall of Freddie the Leaf* (Holt, 1982) is a good one to read to grieving students. *A Taste of Blackberries* by Doris B. Smith (Crowell Junior, 1973) is another good one. It is about Jamie, who dies of a bee sting. His best friend is confronted with the loss and feels guilty because somehow he should have saved Jamie. Hannelore Wass, professor at the University of Florida, has written several books on death, which contain annotated lists of books and audiovisual materials on the topic for both children and adults (see Wass citations in the References).

If a student seeks you out and wants to talk, LISTEN with your ears, eyes, and heart. You cannot protect students from experiencing the pain of a classmate's death, but you can help them cope. You can help them to understand their feelings and to restore their self-worth. Kids are resilient. If they were well adjusted before the tragedy, most will be okay; and from the experience they will grow and learn.

Teacher Suggestions for the Formal Operational Stage

By adolescence students are in the formal operations stage. They can think logically and abstractly. They are developing a sense of morality. Their concepts about death are much like those of adults. But adolescence is also a time of intense emotional conflicts as students try to establish their identity and independence and deal with peer pressure. At this age a classmate's death can only exacerbate what is already a highly stressful stage of life.

Moreover, the departmentalized structure of secondary schools, where students change classes and teachers every hour, does not provide the family-like atmosphere of the self-contained elementary classroom. It is more difficult to deal with the trauma of a student death in the secondary school setting. This difficulty is captured in the following incident, which a school counselor shared with the author.

A popular eighth-grade boy had been killed while riding his bike home from school. No plans were made on how to cope with the tragedy the next day at school. One teacher talked quietly with her class, telling them of her sadness. The math teacher's reaction was, "Let's get to work; life must go on." The language arts teacher cried the whole day, and the students in her classes either cried or sat morosely for 45 minutes. The math teacher who said "life must go on" chastized the teacher who cried all day for "getting the kids all upset." In this atmosphere of mixed signals, the students were the losers.

Announcing the news of a student death in the first-period class or homeroom class is preferable to using the public address system or bringing students together in the auditorium. In the smaller classroom setting, teachers can respond to students' questions and attend to their emotional needs.

Present the facts of the tragedy as completely as possible. If complete information is not yet available, tell the student that you will give them an update as soon as you have further information. Alert students not to give credence to rumor. Tell them to challenge all statements that begin with "I heard that . . ." When information is lacking, they must assume nothing.

Adolescents will react to the news in different ways. After the initial shock, students may exhibit anger, fear, and depression. Emotional outbursts are common and are "contagious" at this age level. Allow students to talk about their feelings and to share their grief with each other.

Designate a place at school where students may go to express their grief. Students close to the deceased may be too upset to go to class. The school library could be closed and used as a place for students to go to cry, talk, or just sit.

Have available a list of counselors, community agencies, and crisis hot lines to which students in need of personal counseling can be referred.

A memorial service for the deceased student helps to bring about healing and closure of the grieving process.

When the Grieving Student Returns

School had become a disaster for 15-year-old Selena. Her older sister, a teacher, had been shot by her own husband, who mistook her for an intruder in their bedroom in the middle of the night. In the weeks following this bizarre tragedy, Selena could not concentrate. Her emotions ranged from hysteria to anger; she often wanted to be alone. Fortunately for Selena, she had someone to turn to when she needed to talk about her feelings. It was her English teacher, who is also a grief counselor. She was trained in a program in Jacksonville, Florida, directed by Jessica Gurvitt.

As director of a hospice in Jacksonville, Gurvitt received many calls from teachers asking for help with students who were not adjusting after the death of a family member. This prompted her to develop a training program for teachers and counselors to help grieving students. The 10-week training program, called "Children and Grief: Living with Loss," is now used in many schools nationwide and has won several awards. Grieving students meet with trained teachers individually and attend a group session once a week. The student may ask for a pass to talk to the teacher when necessary. Said Gurvitt, "The main thing you are providing them with is an outlet."

Like Selena, bereaved students returning to school will not bounce right back into the swing of things. Grief symptoms are not left at home; it takes time for grief to be resolved.

The grieving student, on returning to school, may exhibit a variety of symptoms ranging from disruption of regular habit patterns to depression episodes to psychosomatic disorders. Mary Spaid (n.d.) of the Ocala (Florida) Hospice has compiled a long list of physiological and behavioral responses found in bereaved students:

Physiological responses:
- Increased heart rate
- Increased adrenalin flow
- High blood pressure
- Gastric upset
- Feelings of exhaustion
- Restlessness
- Aches and pains
- Hyperventilation
- Sighing
- Headaches
- Lack of concentration
- Lower resistance to disease

Behavioral responses:
- Crying episodes
- Increased sensitivity
- Temper tantrums
- Clinging
- Detachment, withdrawal, and indifference to events
- Changes in eating patterns (overeating, lack of appetite)
- Changes in sleeping patterns (insomnia, wake up often, sleep too long)
- Changes in elimination patterns (bedwetting, constipation, diarrhea)
- Changes in school performance (failing, dropping out, overachieving)
- Regression to earlier behaviors (thumbsucking, use of nightlight)

- Compulsive, ritualistic acts
- Risk-taking (speeding or hazardous stunts)
- Aggressiveness, acting out
- Alcohol, drug abuse

When the grieving student returns to school, a sensitive teacher or counselor can help by using the technique of "active listening." The technique involves:

1. Reflecting, that is, using a question to help the student articulate more fully what they are feeling or are concerned about.
2. Being aware of the student's cognitive developmental level. (Recall the kindergartner who asked, "When is Jenny coming back?" At his cognitive level death is reversible.)
3. Responding in a timely fashion to a question or comment rather than averting it.
4. Giving an honest response that will increase a child's understanding about death without developing fears or fostering fantasies. A child's question about the burial service, "Will the dirt get on her face?" calls for a straightforward answer: "No, the lid of the casket will be closed and sealed. Dirt cannot get in."
5. Provide emotional support.

The following dialogue illustrates the above technique.

Child: I hate God. *(Teacher doesn't show shock or scold child for making such a statement.)*

Teacher: When we lose someone we really love, we feel angry and think we hate someone. Are you feeling angry with God because your mother died in the car wreck? *(Teacher uses reflective question.)*

Child: Yes, I am. I hate him for letting this happen. *(The cognitive level of the child comes through here as he attempts to determine cause.)*

Teacher: It's okay to feel angry. If you let yourself feel angry, then after a while the anger will go away. *(Teacher answers in a timely fashion.)*

Child: But maybe I'll be punished for being angry at God. *(The child expresses guilt for such feelings and fears punishment.)*

Teacher: I think God is big enough to handle your anger. God will understand how you feel about the loss of your mother. *(The teacher provides emotional support and has increased the child's understanding of life and death.)*

Sometimes students mourn at a distance. They may show little emotion at the time of a sibling's death but have tremendous empathy for a character in a book who dies. Other students mask or cover up their real feelings. A girl returned to school the day after her brother's funeral (he had died suddenly of an aortic aneurysm). She was talking and laughing with her friends in the school parking lot when one of her teachers came by and confronted her, saying, "Aren't you ashamed of yourself laughing when you just buried your brother yesterday." The girl cried all day at school and threatened never to come back because of the insensitive comment of the teacher.

Friends and classmates are often at a loss as to what to say to bereaved students when they return to school. In most cases the best advice you can give students is to say simply, "I'm so sorry." Caution them to avoid such clichés as "I know how you feel" (to the grieving person, you cannot possibly know how they feel) or "It will all work out, you will soon be able to forget" (the grieving person does not want to forget). Most bereaved persons report that it is the expression of concern they remember, not the specific words.

Conclusion

Dealing with death is never easy, but it is part of life. The "strategy for tragedy" presented in this fastback offers many suggestions for consideration when a student death occurs. A school might want to consider an inservice program on death and grieving covering the following topics:

1. Teachers becoming aware of their own attitudes toward death. The Leming Death Fear Scale (Leming and Dickinson 1985) is useful in this regard. It consists of a 26-item questionnaire that asks individuals to rank their fears and concerns and then groups these for subsequent discussion.

2. Knowledge of student bereavement behavior. Many teachers do not realize the range of behaviors that students exhibit when a relative or classmate dies or how long the grieving process can go on. By becoming familiar with these behaviors, teachers can better determine if professional help is needed.

3. Knowledge of children's cognitive development with regard to concepts about death. If teachers are to help the grieving child, they need to understand children's perceptions of death from preschool through adolescence.

4. Knowledge of available resources. Many printed and audiovisual resources are available (see References). Local resources include counselors trained in grief counseling, hospice staff, and grief support groups. A local college or university may offer a course in death education.

With the knowledge and skills learned in a well-planned inservice program, teachers will be prepared to help their students in a sensitive and compassionate manner. Life does go on after the loss of a loved one, but the rocky road can be made smoother when there is a strategy for tragedy.

References

The Compassionate Friends (a support group for parents whose child has died). National office: Box 1347, Oakbrook, IL 60521.

Cohn, Janice. "The Grieving Student." *Instructor* 96 (January 1987): 76-78. (Cohn founded the Helping Children in Crisis program at the New York Center for Crisis Service, 305 West End Avenue, Suite 14F, New York, NY 10023.)

Crase, Darrell, and Hamrick, M. "The Imperative for a National Initiative in Death-Related Phenomena." *Journal of School Health* 59 (February 1989): 79-80.

Franson, Joseph. "Coping with the Trauma of a Violent Death." *NASSP Bulletin* 72 (October 1988): 88-91.

Gordon, A., and Klaus, D. *They Need to Know: How to Teach Children About Death*. Englewood Cliffs, N.J.: Prentice-Hall, 1979.

Gurvitt, Jessica. *Children and Grief: Living with Loss*. This program is available from P.O. Box 50399, Jacksonville Beach, FL 32240-0399. Phone: (904) 241-2182.

Harris, Janet. *Your Grief: You're Not Going Crazy*. Mothers Against Drunk Driving, 1985. (MADD, 669 Airport Fwy., Suite 310, Hurst, TX 76053.)

Karioth, Sally. *If You Want to Know You're Dying, Ask the Cleaning Lady*. Tallahassee, Fla.: K.P., 1985. (Karioth is a popular speaker at seminars and conferences. Her address is 2406 Mexia Avenue, Tallahassee, FL 32304.)

Kastenbaum, R. *Death, Society, and Human Experience*. St. Louis: C.V. Mosby, 1981.

Leming, R., and Dickinson, G. *Understanding Dying, Death, and Bereavement*. New York: Holt, Rhinehart and Winston, 1985.

Oaks, Judy, and Bibeau, Daniel. "Death Education: Educating Children for Living." *Clearing House* 60 (May 1987): 420-22.

Pratt, Clara; Hare, Jan; and Wright, Cheryl. "Death and Dying in Early Childhood Education: Are Educators Prepared?" *Education* 107 (Spring 1987): 279-86.

Marion County (Florida) Psychological Services. "Crisis Response Team Memorandum," 14 August 1989. (P.O. Box 690, Ocala, FL 32678.)

Sinkkonen, Mary. "Responding Sensitively to Tragedy." *Thrust* 18 (May-June 1989): 22.

Spaid, Mary K. "Constructive Strategies for Helping Children to Understand and Accept Loss." Ocala (Florida) Hospice (undated and unpublished). Available from the Ocala Hospice, P.O. Box 4860, Ocala, FL 32678-4860.

Wass, Hannelore, and Corr, Charles. *Helping Children Cope with Death: Guideline and Resources*. Washington D.C.: Hemisphere, 1984.

Wass, Hannelore, et. al. *Death Education: An Annotated Resource Guide*. Washington D.C.: Hemisphere, 1984.

Wass, H., and Sullivan, J. "Death in the Lives of Children and Adolescents." In *Dying: Facing the Facts*, 2nd ed., edited by Wass, Berado, and Niemeyer. Washington, D.C.: Hemisphere, 1988.